OCCASIONAL PAPER

The Option of an Oil Tax to Fund Transportation and Infrastructure

Keith Crane • *Nicholas Burger* • *Martin Wachs*

INVESTMENT IN PEOPLE AND IDEAS

This paper results from the RAND Corporation's Investment in People and Ideas program. Support for this program is provided, in part, by the generosity of RAND's donors and by the fees earned on client-funded research. This research was conducted in the Environment, Energy, and Economic Development Program (EEED) within RAND Infrastructure, Safety, and Environment (ISE).

Library of Congress Cataloging-in-Publication Data

Crane, Keith, 1953-
  The option of an oil tax to fund transportation and infrastructure / Keith Crane, Nicholas Burger, Martin Wachs.
      p. cm.
  Includes bibliographical references.
  ISBN 978-0-8330-5178-3 (pbk. : alk. paper)
  1. Petroleum--Taxation—Economic aspects—United States. I. Burger, Nicholas. II. Wachs, Martin. III. Title.

  HD9560.8.U52C73 2011
  336.2'785532820973—dc22

                                                                            2011005695

The RAND Corporation is a nonprofit institution that helps improve policy and decisionmaking through research and analysis. RAND's publications do not necessarily reflect the opinions of its research clients and sponsors.

RAND® is a registered trademark.

Published 2011 by the RAND Corporation
1776 Main Street, P.O. Box 2138, Santa Monica, CA 90407-2138
1200 South Hayes Street, Arlington, VA 22202-5050
4570 Fifth Avenue, Suite 600, Pittsburgh, PA 15213-2665
RAND URL: http://www.rand.org/
To order RAND documents or to obtain additional information, contact
Distribution Services: Telephone: (310) 451-7002;
Fax: (310) 451-6915; Email: order@rand.org

Preface

There is increasing concern in the U.S. Congress about long-term federal transportation funding. This paper is designed to assist policymakers in assessing whether an oil tax would be a useful option for funding future expenditures on U.S. transportation infrastructure. It assesses the costs and benefits of replacing current U.S. vehicular fuel taxes and other transportation taxes with a percentage tax on each barrel of oil consumed in the United States. The rate used for such a tax would fluctuate, falling as oil prices rise and rising as oil prices fall, but would be set so that sufficient tax revenues are raised to meet targets set by Congress. The paper evaluates who would likely pay the tax (consumers, refiners, or oil producers) and how proceeds of the tax might be used. This paper is part of the RAND Corporation's larger body of research and analysis on energy and the environment, especially work focused on informing new policy directions.

This paper results from RAND's Investment in People and Ideas program. Support for this program is provided, in part, by the generosity of RAND's donors and by the fees earned on client-funded research.

The RAND Environment, Energy, and Economic Development Program

This research was conducted in the Environment, Energy, and Economic Development Program (EEED) within RAND Infrastructure, Safety, and Environment (ISE). The mission of RAND Infrastructure, Safety, and Environment is to improve the development, operation, use, and protection of society's essential physical assets and natural resources and to enhance the related social assets of safety and security of individuals in transit and in their workplaces and communities. The EEED research portfolio addresses environmental quality and regulation, energy resources and systems, water resources and systems, climate, natural hazards and disasters, and economic development—both domestically and internationally. EEED research is conducted for government, foundations, and the private sector.

Questions or comments about this paper should be sent to the project leader, Keith Crane (Keith_Crane@rand.org). Information about the Environment, Energy, and Economic Development Program is available online (http://www.rand.org/ise/environ). Inquiries about EEED projects should be sent to the following address:

Keith Crane, Director
Environment, Energy, and Economic Development Program, ISE
RAND Corporation
1200 South Hayes Street
Arlington, VA 22202-5050
703-413-1100, x5520
Keith_Crane@rand.org

Contents

Figures

Tables

Summary

The goal of this paper is to raise the key issues associated with using an oil tax to fund U.S. transportation infrastructure, identify the decisions Congress would need to make in designing such a tax, and outline some of the likely implications of adopting an oil tax. In 2009, federal spending on surface-transportation infrastructure outpaced revenues into the federal Highway Trust Fund (HTF) by $18.6 billion. The HTF is funded through federal taxes on gasoline and diesel fuel. Because these taxes are not indexed to inflation and because U.S. motor vehicles are becoming more efficient, resulting in fewer purchases of gasoline and diesel, real revenue generated from these taxes has declined. Congress is considering ways to address this gap between transportation revenues and expenditures.

In this paper, we investigate using a percentage tax on crude oil and imported refined petroleum products consumed in the United States to fund the nation's transportation infrastructure. This proposed tax on oil could replace existing gasoline and diesel taxes and, potentially, other transportation taxes, such as taxes on airline tickets. The revenues from this tax could be used to fully fund federal infrastructure expenditures on highways, public transit, and aviation.

A percentage tax on oil would have several advantages over existing transportation funding systems. It could simplify the tax system by replacing several existing taxes used to finance transportation with a single, upstream tax. It could be adjusted automatically to fully fund appropriated expenditures on transportation, regardless of inflation. It could transfer external costs of producing and consuming oil that are currently borne by the general public to be borne only by oil producers and consumers. It would spread the burden of these external costs across all users of petroleum products, not just motorists and truckers. It could help fund national security expenditures employed to safeguard sources and sea-lanes used to import oil. Finally, while the public is generally opposed to most taxes, given the national security concerns associated with oil consumption, an oil tax might be more politically palatable than raising existing motor fuel taxes.

In the paper, we provide revenue estimates based on different potential oil tax rates at various oil prices. We then match potential revenues to estimates of transportation expenditure needs. At mid-summer 2010 prices of $72 per barrel, an oil tax of 17 percent would generate approximately $83 billion per year, the projected annual federal appropriation for ground-transit infrastructure over the next six years.[1] The hypothetical oil tax would be collected at

---

[1] As we describe in more detail below, our primary results assume no short-term demand or supply response to higher oil taxes. Long-run revenue-generation potential would need to account for demand reductions due to higher prices; we provide general estimates of the long-run effect of higher oil prices on demand.

refineries, with separate adjustments for imported and exported refined petroleum products. The tax would need to be flexible to balance revenue needs with the economic burden of the tax. One option is to adjust the tax rate quarterly to account for changes in the price of oil, maintaining annual revenues but reducing the percentage tax take if oil prices spike once again.

We also provide an estimate of the aggregate "external" costs associated with producing and consuming oil, costs an oil tax could help to internalize. These external costs include damage to health and the environment from pollution associated with oil, costs associated with climate change, economic declines stemming from disruptions in the supply of oil, and national security–related costs. Because consumers and producers do not face most of these costs—even though society pays them—decisions about consuming refined oil products are not economically efficient. An oil tax could be designed to better price oil resources, leading to more efficient use of this resource.

Some users, including motorists and truckers, would likely see only modest increases in total taxes paid if a tax on oil replaced current taxes on gasoline and diesel. However, other users of refined oil products—such as people who heat their homes with fuel oil—would pay federal taxes on petroleum products where they had paid none before. Because energy taxes are regressive, low-income consumers or consumers in certain geographic regions, such as the Northeast, would likely be affected more by an oil tax than higher-income consumers or those living in more moderate climates.

Congress would have a number of options for choosing how to allocate the revenues of an oil tax to pay for transportation infrastructure. These include using existing mechanisms, such as the HTF, or abandoning the current "user pays" system in favor of general-fund financing. If revenue from an optimal tax were higher than the level required to fund transportation expenditures, Congress could offset the likely regressive effects of an energy tax by reducing other distortionary taxes, such as payroll taxes.[2]

We also acknowledge the paper's limitations. A full, quantitative analysis of the costs and benefits of an oil tax is beyond our scope, although we do provide quantitative estimates where possible. We also do not attempt to calculate the "optimal" oil tax, one that would balance revenue generation, internalizing external costs, and tax interaction effects. Although we discuss the possible effects of a federal oil tax on oil prices, our analysis does not consider in detail the broader general equilibrium effects of significant changes in the U.S. tax system. The intended audience is national policymakers considering alternative transportation financing options. We acknowledge that additional analysis would be necessary to choose the parameters of an actual tax on oil and assess its implications.

---

[2]   Distortionary taxes are taxes that cause people to change their behavior in a socially costly way.

Acknowledgments

We thank Frank Camm, David Ortiz, Steven Popper, Constantine Samaras, and the staff at the office of U.S. Representative John Garamendi for valuable feedback. We also recognize the contributions and recommendations from our two reviewers, Kenneth Small and Johanna Zmud. Any errors and omissions remain our own.

Abbreviations

Btu	British thermal unit
CAFE	Corporate Average Fuel Economy
CO	carbon monoxide
CO_2	carbon dioxide
HTF	Highway Trust Fund
mpg	mile per gallon
NOx	nitrogen oxide
PM	particulate matter
SO_2	sulfur dioxide
SOx	sulfur oxide
VMT	vehicle mile traveled

Introduction

Highway expenditures in the United States are increasing while revenues from traditional funding sources, taxes on gasoline and diesel, are declining (Figure 1). As Americans continue to drive, but motor vehicles become more fuel efficient, this funding gap will continue to widen, presenting Congress with the challenge of how to reliably fund transportation infrastructure.

Each year, U.S. citizens incur a number of real, if unseen, costs associated with the consumption of gasoline and diesel and, by extension, oil. These range from environmental pollution stemming from the consumption of gasoline and diesel fuel to macroeconomic instability from oil price shocks to national security costs related to oil production by unfriendly regimes. Because these costs are external to consumers, the price of gasoline, diesel, and other oil-based products does not accurately reflect the true cost of oil consumption. An oil tax—imposed on petroleum and petroleum products consumed in the United States—is one way to simultaneously provide a reliable source of funding for U.S. transportation infrastructure and ensure that the price of oil more accurately reflects its true costs.

Figure 1
Highway Trust Fund Revenues and U.S. Federal Government Expenditures on Ground Transportation in Constant 2009 Dollars (1977–2009)

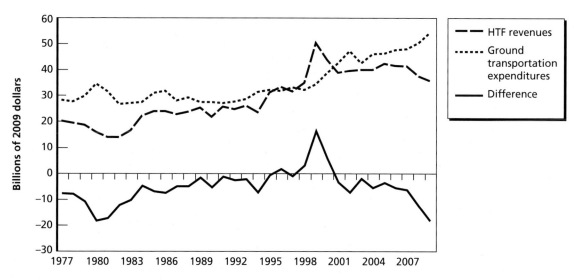

SOURCE: Office of Management and Budget, 2011a, 2011b.
NOTE: HTF = Highway Trust Fund.
RAND OP320-1

1

In this paper, we present one option for a federal oil tax and estimate potential revenue streams that might be generated by such a tax. We also identify and describe—quantitatively where feasible—the various costs associated with oil consumption that are not currently paid by consumers of oil. An oil tax is an effective mechanism through which to shift these costs from the public at large to those who impose these costs on society. The oil tax we propose is a percentage tax that would be periodically adjusted to reflect changes in the price of oil so that sufficient revenues are generated to cover government expenditures and external costs. It would be designed to rise with inflation and to increase to cover increased costs of federally funded roads and surface transportation, while not overly burdening consumers when oil prices rise. We also discuss potential distributional implications for the tax, including how the burden would be shared between consumers and producers, how much of the tax foreign producers might bear, and which income and geographic groups would be likely to pay the tax.

The paper is organized as follows: The next section introduces the concept of an oil tax as a mechanism to fund federal spending on transportation. It discusses a design for such a tax. Section 3 explores the potential types of expenditures an oil tax would fund and describes the external costs associated with oil consumption. In the last section, we discuss who would pay for an oil tax, focusing on income and distributional effects, and discuss implications for federal transportation funding.

Why Tax Oil?

Gasoline and Diesel Taxes Are Insufficient to Pay for Roads

The U.S. federal government and the states finance most expenditures on roads and some on public transportation by taxing gasoline and diesel fuel. Revenues from federal taxes flow into the federal HTF, which includes a transit account. Federal transportation appropriations are paid to the states through disbursements from the trust fund.

Federal taxes on gasoline and diesel are $0.184 and $0.244 per gallon, respectively. They have not been raised since 1993 (Energy Information Administration, 2010a). Since the federal gasoline tax was last increased, the purchasing power of the dollar as measured by the consumer price index has fallen by one-third. In addition to the effects of inflation, as cars and trucks have become more fuel efficient, they travel farther on a gallon of gasoline or diesel fuel.[1] Federal HTF revenues per mile driven have fallen dramatically as better fuel economy translates into fewer gallons of fuel purchased. As a consequence of the effects of inflation and improved fuel economy, federal fuel taxes are no longer sufficient to cover the costs of federal highway programs. In 2008, HTF revenues ran $36.4 billion; expenditures ran $49.2 billion. In 2009, revenues fell as expenditures rose: Inflation-adjusted HTF revenues from taxes on gasoline and diesel fuel fell to 30 percent below their 1999 peak (Office of Management and Budget, 2011a).

Figure 2 shows prices of gasoline and federal gasoline taxes over time.[2] In 2008, the federal tax constituted 5.5 percent of the cost of a gallon of regular gasoline, substantially less (40 percent) than the average share of federal taxes in the price of gasoline in the 1990s (13.9 percent).

Revenues from gasoline and diesel taxes will continue to decline once adjusted for inflation. The U.S. federal government has mandated further improvements in the fuel economy of cars and light trucks under Corporate Average Fuel Economy (CAFE) standards. By 2016, manufacturers will be required to achieve average corporate fuel economy of 37.8 miles per gallon (mpg) for cars and 28.8 mpg for trucks, up from 27.5 mpg for cars and 23.5 mpg in 2010 (National Highway Traffic Safety Administration, undated). Between 2010 and 2016, improvements in fuel efficiency will lead to annual average declines of 5.2 and 3.3 percent in average fuel consumption per mile for new cars and light trucks, respectively. Between 1993 and 2007, the last prerecession year, the number of vehicle miles traveled (VMT) in the United

---

[1] Fuel efficiency for new cars has increased from an average of 24.3 miles per gallon in 1980 to 32.6 miles per gallon in 2009 (Bureau of Transportation Statistics, undated [b]).

[2] Raw data are provided in the appendix.

Figure 2
Gasoline Prices and Taxes: 1949–2008

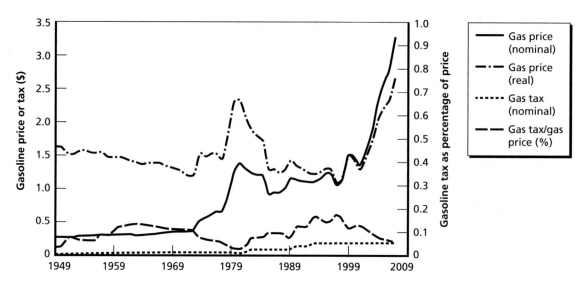

SOURCES: Gasoline tax data from "When Did the Federal Government Begin Collecting the Gas Tax?" 2005; gasoline price data from Energy Information Administration, 2010b.
RAND OP320-2

States rose at an average annual rate of 1.6 percent (Federal Highway Administration, 2009). Even if increases in VMT return to prerecession rates, improvements in fuel economy are likely to result in declines in the consumption of gasoline and diesel fuel and hence revenues from fuel taxes. Efforts to introduce plug-in hybrids or to use biofuels, which presently are untaxed, could result in even lower revenues.

While revenues from fuel taxes have fallen, costs of building and repairing roads have risen.[3] Limited HTF revenues have, by necessity, been channeled into road repair rather than new capacity. As a consequence, over the past three decades, the United States has added very little capacity to its road network, while VMT rose 95 percent between 1980 and 2008 (Bureau of Transportation Statistics, undated [a]). During this same period, congestion has increased markedly. At least some of this congestion could be reduced by investments in roads and public transportation, in addition to such policies as fuel taxes.

Legislators Have Been Unwilling to Raise Gasoline and Diesel Taxes

Antitax sentiment has made legislators reluctant to raise the per-gallon tax on motor fuels, especially when the price of gasoline is high. The federal government and some states have responded by turning to general revenues, levying other dedicated taxes, or issuing bonds to finance roads.

The shift to general revenues is contrary to traditional practice. For decades, taxpayers have considered gasoline and diesel taxes to be "user fees" for roads and transportation. Through these taxes, those who use the roads bear their costs. When roads and public trans-

---

[3] For example, while the Consumer Price Index rose by 870 percent between 1949 and 2008, the Construction Cost Index rose 1,700 percent over the same period (Grogan, 2010).

portation are funded out of general revenues, they compete for funding against schools, police, and parks at the state level, and against defense, health care, and other expenditures at the federal level.

A shift away from the practice of "user pays" is likely to lead to more use of roads and less investment. Current transportation taxes and fees are insufficient to ensure that drivers pay the full costs of using roads. By decoupling road use from taxes, fuel is cheaper for drivers and truckers than it otherwise would be. This reduces incentives to restrain driving and contributes to more congestion. Moreover, general revenue support for transportation infrastructure might be less reliable than dedicated funds, leading to insufficient funding for roads and other transportation infrastructure.

Design and Benefits of a Tax on Oil

A tax on oil would encounter some of the same antitax concerns that have made Congress unwilling to raise federal gasoline and diesel taxes. However, the public might be more willing to support a tax on oil in lieu of raising motor fuel taxes or as a substitute for these taxes. The American public has long been concerned about national security risks associated with oil consumption; this concern has engendered support in some quarters for measures designed to reduce dependence on oil—especially imported oil (Deutch, Schlesinger, and Victor, 2006). However, because a tax on oil would necessarily affect a large number of interest groups, including groups with active and effective lobbying power, the political challenges facing a proposed oil tax are likely to be significant.

In light of opposition to raising federal gasoline taxes, one option for covering increased costs of maintaining and improving our roads and transportation infrastructure would be to replace fixed-rate taxes on gasoline and diesel fuel with a percentage tax on each barrel of oil consumed in the United States. We argue that the percentage rate levied under this tax should be flexible: It should be set so as to ensure adequate revenues for surface transportation and other expenditures deemed to be tied to U.S. oil consumption. This percentage should be adjusted on an annual or quarterly basis to ensure that sufficient revenues are available but that consumers are not penalized during periods when prices spike. Accordingly, when oil prices rise, the tax rate would fall so that consumers and businesses are not doubly penalized by both higher oil prices and higher taxes. Conversely, when oil prices fall, the tax rate would rise, ensuring that sufficient revenues are available to cover the cost of roads.

The tax would probably best be collected at the refinery. To ensure that the domestic refining industry faces a level international playing field, imports of refined petroleum products would incur a tax equivalent to that on oil. To preserve their competitiveness, exporters of refined petroleum products would receive a tax rebate equivalent to the tax on the crude oil used to produce the exported products.

There are multiple advantages to employing a graduated percentage tax on oil as opposed to fixed per-gallon taxes on gasoline and diesel. First, one of the greatest problems with the current tax is that it is not adjusted for inflation. Road construction costs rise over time, but the tax does not. Revenues from a graduated percentage tax would increase as oil prices rise, and the percentage rate could be automatically adjusted to ensure that a sufficient level of revenue for transportation funding is available if prices drop.

Second, the tax could replace several other taxes, potentially simplifying the tax system. If the proposed tax were adopted, excise taxes on gasoline, diesel fuel, and aviation fuel all could be eliminated, reducing the number of transportation taxes collected.

Third, an oil tax could be designed to internalize various external costs associated with the production and consumption of petroleum products. As so vividly demonstrated by the recent oil spill in the Gulf of Mexico, producing oil imposes environmental costs. Consuming oil also imposes environmental and human health costs. An oil tax that incorporates the costs of damage to the environment would allow consumers and producers to make decisions based on prices that reflect the full environmental costs of their activities. On the other hand, to the extent that different transportation modes impose different external costs (as discussed in Section 3), a single tax would be less effective than differentiated taxes in providing proper signals to consumers of gasoline and diesel concerning the real costs of their behavior.

In addition to environmental costs, imported oil from unstable or unfriendly states imposes national security costs on the United States. Abrupt cutoffs in the global supply of oil, no matter the source, would trigger a sharp rise in world oil prices, potentially harming the U.S. economy. By imposing a tax on oil, the U.S. government would tap into a stream of revenues that would defray some of the costs of preserving economic stability in the event of a surge in oil prices. For example, the tax could be designed to cover the cost of stocking and maintaining the Strategic Petroleum Reserve.

Since the presidency of Jimmy Carter, U.S. armed forces have been tasked with defending sources of oil and the transportation routes along which oil is shipped. The cost of this mission is significant. In line with sound economic principles, the cost of this service could be incorporated into the price of oil through a tax yielding an offsetting amount of revenue.

An oil tax would be more broadly based than taxes on specific transportation fuels. An oil tax, as opposed to taxes on just gasoline and diesel, would spread the burden of environmental and national security costs across all consumers of petroleum products, including home heating oil and petroleum coke. A tax imposed on all oil products ensures that tax policies do not distort the development of new technologies by encouraging the substitution of other refined oil products for diesel and gasoline.

How Much Might Oil Be Taxed?

A key challenge to implementing a percentage tax on petroleum is setting appropriate tax rates. In any one period, the rate needs to be set so that it generates sufficient revenues to fund appropriate levels of federal spending on transportation. We argue that rates should also be set so that they address the external costs associated with oil consumption. In this section, we discuss the tax rates needed to generate revenues sufficient to fund current proposals for spending on ground transportation and describe the various external costs the tax might also be used to cover.

Revenue Needs

In 2009, federal spending on ground transportation ran $53.6 billion, while federal HTF revenues were $34.96 billion (Office of Management and Budget, 2011a). The difference between these expenditures and HTF revenues was financed by federal borrowing. The U.S. House of Representatives Committee on Transportation and Infrastructure is considering a bill to appropriate $450 billion over the next six years for surface transportation and an additional $50 billion for high-speed rail for an annual expenditure of $83 billion. Assuming that U.S. consumption of gasoline and diesel fuel remains at about 2009 levels, to fund this level of expenditure, existing taxes on gasoline and diesel would have to be increased by $0.28 per gallon, increasing the gasoline tax from $0.184 to $0.46 per gallon and that on diesel from $0.244 to $0.52 per gallon.

In 2009, the United States consumed 6,865,650,000 barrels of oil or oil-equivalent fuel products (Energy Information Administration [EIA], 2010a, Table A11), purchased at an average price of about $59.04 per barrel of oil (EIA, 2010a, Table A12), for a total expenditure of $405 billion.[1] If all federal taxes on gasoline and diesel were eliminated and replaced with a percentage tax on oil, in 2009, a 9-percent tax on the value of a barrel of oil would have generated the same amount of revenue for the federal HTF as current taxes do on gasoline and diesel fuel. Assuming that U.S. oil consumption remains flat and oil prices average $72 per barrel, roughly the price of oil at mid-summer, sufficient revenues ($83 billion) could be raised to fund federal surface-transportation programs with a percentage tax of approximately 17 percent.[2] In

---

[1] Annualized daily consumption of 18.85 million barrels. Price is the average imported oil price for 2009. For comparison, average West Texas Intermediate price for 2009 was $61.66 (EIA, 2011).

[2] The spot price for oil was $72.14 on July 2, 2010, for West Texas Intermediate (EIA, undated).

the long run, oil demand would respond to higher prices from an oil tax, and higher tax rates would likely be needed to achieve revenue targets. We address this point further in Section 4.

Different percentage taxes and various oil prices would generate a wide range of revenues. Table 1 illustrates potential revenue streams for a variety of price points and levels of taxation assuming 2009 oil-consumption levels.

For example, a tax on oil could be set at a level to cover federal spending on air transportation as well as on surface transportation. U.S. revenues from taxes on air travel were $10.6 billion in 2009. If a tax on oil were to be substituted for these taxes, it would have to be set at 19 percent at a price of $72 per barrel to cover all expenditures on transportation, 2 percentage points more than a tax set just to cover federal expenditures on ground transportation.

As we discuss in more detail in Section 4, higher oil prices would lead to a drop in the amount of oil demanded in the long run. As a result, the tax rates presented in Table 1 might not reflect the long-run revenue potential for an oil tax, since the total oil consumed would fall, reducing the total tax revenue generated. In Table 2, we present revenue numbers based on how consumers might respond to higher oil prices. The "long-run" revenues reflect reduced demand for oil—based on a −0.3 elasticity—from higher prices.[3] For any given oil price and tax rate combination, the long-run revenues are smaller than the short-run revenues; for example, a tax of approximately 19 percent would be needed to generate $83 billion in revenue, the amount needed to fund near-term transportation expenditures. Although the long-run revenue

Table 1
Revenue Projections from a Percentage Tax on a Barrel of Oil at Varying Prices and Percentage Rates of Taxation, Assuming 2009 U.S. Oil Consumption Levels

Oil Price per Barrel (2009 dollars)	Revenue at Each Percentage Tax Level (billions of 2009 dollars)								
	9%	12%	15%	18%	21%	24%	27%	30%	33%
40	24.7	33.0	41.2	49.4	57.7	65.9	74.1	82.4	90.6
50	30.9	41.2	51.5	61.8	72.1	82.4	92.7	103.0	113.3
60	37.1	49.4	61.8	74.1	86.5	98.9	111.2	123.6	135.9
70	43.2	57.7	72.1	86.5	100.9	115.3	129.7	144.2	158.6
80	49.4	65.9	82.4	98.9	115.3	131.8	148.3	164.8	181.2
90	55.6	74.1	92.7	111.2	129.7	148.3	166.8	185.4	203.9
100	61.8	82.4	103.0	123.6	144.2	164.8	185.3	206.0	226.5
110	68.0	90.6	113.3	135.9	158.6	181.2	203.9	226.6	249.2
120	74.1	98.9	123.6	148.3	173.0	197.7	222.4	247.2	271.8
130	80.3	107.1	133.9	160.6	187.4	214.2	240.9	267.8	294.5
140	86.5	115.3	144.2	173.0	201.8	230.7	259.5	288.4	317.1
150	92.7	123.6	154.5	185.3	216.2	247.1	278.0	309.0	339.8

NOTE: Assumes 2009 consumption levels of approximately 6.87 billion barrels of oil. We assume no demand response (i.e., short-term revenue).

---

[3]   See the note in the table for key assumptions and limitations.

Table 2
Revenue Projections from a Percentage Tax on a Barrel of Oil at Varying Prices and Percentage Rates of Taxation, Assuming 2009 U.S. Oil Consumption Levels with Demand Response from Consumers

Oil Price per Barrel (2009 dollars)	Revenue at Each Percentage Tax Level (billions of 2009 dollars)								
	9% (6.68)	12% (6.62)	15% (6.56)	18% (6.49)	21% (6.43)	24% (6.37)	27% (6.31)	30% (6.25)	33% (6.19)
40	24.0	31.8	39.3	46.8	54.0	61.2	68.1	75.0	81.6
50	30.1	39.7	49.2	58.4	67.5	76.4	85.2	93.7	102.1
60	36.1	47.6	59.0	70.1	81.0	91.7	102.2	112.4	122.5
70	42.1	55.6	68.8	81.8	94.6	107.0	119.2	131.2	142.9
80	48.1	63.5	78.7	93.5	108.1	122.3	136.3	149.9	163.3
90	54.1	71.5	88.5	105.2	121.6	137.6	153.3	168.7	183.7
100	60.1	79.4	98.3	116.9	135.1	152.9	170.3	187.4	204.1
110	66.1	87.4	108.2	128.6	148.6	168.2	187.4	206.1	224.5
120	72.1	95.3	118.0	140.3	162.1	183.5	204.4	224.9	244.9
130	78.1	103.2	127.8	152.0	175.6	198.8	221.4	243.6	265.3
140	84.2	111.2	137.7	163.6	189.1	214.0	238.5	262.4	285.7
150	90.2	119.1	147.5	175.3	202.6	229.3	255.5	281.1	306.2

NOTE: Numbers in parentheses indicate the oil demand, in billions of barrels, at that percentage tax level. We assume 2009 consumption levels of approximately 6.87 billion barrels of oil and demand response based on a long-term elasticity of –0.3. Demand response is independent of initial oil prices, which we acknowledge is a potentially unrealistic assumption; thus, total oil consumption is constant across rows.

potential is important to consider, we focus in the remainder of the paper on short-run revenue generation, since we are motivated by near-term appropriations for highway transportation.

Externalities

In addition to generating revenue for federal government expenditures on transportation, a tax on oil could help to ensure that markets efficiently allocate goods by taxing oil for the unpaid or external costs that oil production and consumption impose on society. External costs, in the case of oil and other goods, are real costs but are typically not incorporated into market prices, leading to greater consumption or production than would be warranted if consumers or producers had to pay the full costs of the product.

In this section, we review costs stemming from environmental damage; where available, we provide quantitative estimates of these costs. We also include costs associated with macroeconomic disruptions and costs pertaining to national security associated with oil. We do not wish to suggest that an oil tax that would generate offsetting revenues for all these costs would be optimal: Calculating a socially optimal tax—a Pigovian tax that accurately reflects all external costs—is beyond the scope of this paper and the data available.[4] Rather, the discussion illustrates—numerically, when feasible—some of the costs associated with oil production and consumption that an oil tax could help reduce.

Damage to the Environment

Extracting oil from the ground and using it to power vehicles, pave roads, and heat homes generates adverse side effects that harm human health and environmental quality. These additional costs are external to the person making the decision to consume oil—they are borne by society. Markets allocate goods and services more efficiently and more equitably when these external costs are internalized—that is, they are shifted to the individuals who are responsible for these costs: producers of oil and consumers of oil products. Here, we review the major environmental externalities associated with petroleum products and, where possible, provide estimates of their economic costs.

Oil Consumption. Refined petroleum products, including gasoline, diesel fuel, aviation fuel, and heating oil, when combusted, produce a variety of airborne pollutants. These include sulfur oxides (SOx), nitrogen oxides (NOx), particulate matter (PM), hydrocarbons, carbon monoxide (CO), and carbon dioxide (CO_2); some pollutants combine to form other air pollution, such as tropospheric ozone. Most of these pollutants have adverse health effects, some of which (e.g., PM and ozone) are especially harmful to at-risk populations, including children and the elderly. Others, such as sulfur dioxide (SO_2), damage crops and have other adverse economic effects.

The use of refined oil products indirectly generates external costs associated with transportation, including congestion and vehicular crashes. Most research on fossil-fuel externalities focuses on roadway congestion and crashes associated with gasoline consumption (e.g., Parry and Small, 2005), but these externalities also apply to transportation-related diesel fuel use and air travel. Congestion imposes significant time costs on all drivers (or aircraft operators) in the congested area, not just the individual driver. In addition, some costs associated with roadway crashes are not borne by the driver and are not taken into account when drivers decide how much to drive—and thus how much oil to consume.[5]

A great deal of research has focused on the external costs of oil or gasoline consumption by passenger vehicles. A recent review paper calculated the external costs associated with gasoline consumption at approximately $2.30 (in 2009 dollars) per gallon (Parry, Walls, and Harrington, 2007).[6] This equates to approximately $44.85 per barrel of oil at current levels of gasoline consumption.[7] However, many of these external costs are associated with the marginal

---

[4]   An optimal tax would be set equal to the marginal external costs associated with oil consumption and production at the *optimal level of consumption*, the level of consumption at which marginal benefits and costs are equal. We do not attempt to calculate the external costs of oil at this level but instead report cost estimates—for a subset of all external costs—at the level of present (or, in some cases, historical) consumption. In addition, an optimal tax based on externalities should be adjusted to incorporate tax interaction effects (e.g., with labor taxes), making externalities only one factor in setting an optimal oil tax.

[5]   For air transport, noise is another sizable external cost not borne by the consumer. However, these costs are difficult to calculate. Because noise pollution is localized, most estimates focus on neighborhoods surrounding specific airports.

[6]   This amount includes local pollution, congestion, and accidents. It does not include geopolitical costs or global warming, which Parry, Walls, and Harrington (2007) also estimate, as we incorporate those costs separately.

[7]   We assume 19.5 gallons of gasoline per barrel of oil. This is based on the typical refining process, which converts a 42-gallon barrel of oil into various refined products, including 19.5 gallons of gasoline. See Figure 3 for more details.

mile driven rather than barrel of oil consumed. An oil tax is unlikely to be the most-efficient way to account for these indirect costs, although, as with gasoline taxes, an oil tax could be a second-best alternative to other more direct taxes, such as congestion surcharges. Policy instruments directly focused on reducing congestion or accidents are likely to be more effective than a tax on oil for addressing these externalities. For example, a congestion tax is a more efficient way to internalize the costs that each driver imposes on others during congested periods. Emissions that damage the environment can be reduced through policies that improve fuel economy or directly reduce pollution per gallon of gasoline combusted. Consequently, under a scenario in which distance-based costs are internalized through alternative policies, we exclude the indirect costs associated with the consumption of oil through passenger travel from our estimates of total external costs.

We know less about the external costs of freight transport, whether by heavy trucks or rail.[8] Like passenger vehicles, these transport modes produce local air pollution, CO_2, noise, congestion, and crashes. In the case of truck travel, there is also the cost of wear and tear on public infrastructure, which might not be internalized by current policies (such as weight restrictions).

There are few estimates of the external costs associated with burning aviation fuel. As with freight travel, much of the pollution produced by airplanes has little effect on human health because it takes place far from population centers. Another significant pollutant produced by aviation, CO_2, is relatively straightforward to internalize through appropriate greenhouse gas charges. Noise, as with automobile transport, is a significant external cost of air transport. But, like road congestion, noise is a function of aircraft characteristics and flight flows and paths, and is highly localized. An oil tax is not the most-efficient way to address these associated costs.

The remaining external costs from oil combustion are those associated with other economic activities for which we consume oil, including home heating, road paving, and finished goods for which petroleum is an input (such as plastics). There are few, if any, estimates of these costs, even though there are cases, such as emissions from asphalt paving, in which costs exist.

Oil Production. The process of exploring for, extracting, and transporting petroleum generates external costs. These range from environmental damage and pollution resulting from oil spills caused by drilling for and extracting oil—as with the Macondo oil spill off the coast of Louisiana—or during transport, such as the oil spill from the *Exxon Valdez* oil tanker. The key issue is the extent to which these costs are borne by oil producers. Some states, such as Alaska, impose surcharges on oil production that are designed to be "environmental taxes," though these are not universal and are relatively low.[9] Oil companies are also liable for the costs of oil spills, although the liability to private parties (noncleanup costs) was capped at $75 million per spill, an amount that would not cover the cost of a major spill. These types of measures help to internalize the external costs of oil production, but, if they are limited or incomplete, they will not fully account for these costs.

Until recently, the literature on the external costs of oil spills focused on spills associated with intra- and international shipping. Spills associated with, for example, offshore drilling, were not typically included in calculations of total costs (see, e.g., Delucchi, 2004). Conse-

---

[8] For a discussion of apportioning the social costs of road travel to freight vehicles, see Delucchi, 1996. Calculating the fraction of total costs attributable to freight travel is beyond the scope of this paper and would not include costs associated with oil consumption by rail; consequently, we have not included estimates based on Delucchi's work.

[9] For example, Alaska collects a $0.04–0.05 "conservation surcharge" on each barrel of oil produced.

quently, existing estimates do not take into account the costs of oil spills from blowouts, such as the spill in the Gulf of Mexico.

Estimating the externalities associated with producing the "marginal" barrel of oil is challenging. Existing policies, such as the Oil Pollution Act of 1990 (Public Law 101-380), make it difficult to use historical data on production risks because these policies internalize some external costs and make it difficult to model the relationship between fuel use and oil spills.[10] Nevertheless, our best estimate of the environmental externalities associated with production is about $0.15 (in 2009 dollars) per barrel (Delucchi, 2000), although we acknowledge that this estimate is out of date. Moreover, Delucchi focuses on tanker-based spills and not, for example, spills associated with deepwater drilling; consequently, this estimate could be considered a lower bound.

Climate Change. A rough estimate of the external costs associated with emissions of CO_2 from burning refined oil products is approximately $5.45 per ton of CO_2 or $2.37 (in 2009 dollars) per barrel (Parry, Walls, and Harrington, 2007; Nordhaus, 2007).[11] However, potential damage to the environment from climate change caused by emissions of CO_2 and other greenhouse gases is more difficult to estimate than environmental damage from localized sources.

Economists have estimated charges (taxes) on CO_2 emissions necessary to substantially reduce emissions in a cost-effective manner. Reductions need to be deep enough and come quickly enough to cause concentrations of greenhouse gases in the atmosphere to stabilize before climate change becomes catastrophic. However, if charges are too high, they might impose substantial economic costs, e.g., scrapping parts of the existing capital stock before they are fully depreciated. This approach differs from calculating the costs of global warming associated with oil consumption, as these estimates focus on inducing changes in technologies and behavior, not estimating discounted economic costs of climate change.

A $30-per-ton tax on CO_2 has been discussed in connection with climate change legislation as a point at which a number of generating technologies (nuclear, wind, biomass, geothermal) might become competitive with coal-fired electricity, the cheapest source of base-load electricity in the United States. Coal-fired power plants are also the largest source of greenhouse gas emissions in the United States. One barrel of oil generates 0.432 metric tons of CO_2. Consequently, imposing a $30-per-ton charge on emissions of CO_2 would be equivalent to a $13 tax per barrel of oil. At a price of $72 per barrel, this would be equivalent to an 18-percent tax on a barrel of oil.

Total Environmental Costs. To calculate total external costs associated with oil consumption and production, one would ideally combine estimates of each cost component for which there are credible estimates (e.g., air pollution, oil spills, climate change). However, there are a number of external costs for which no credible estimate exists; therefore, our estimate of total environmental costs is likely to be on the low side.

From this analysis, we find that one could argue for a tax on oil of as much as $58.00 (high estimates, including local pollution) per barrel or as low as $2.52 per barrel (low estimates, excluding local pollution).[12] The high number incorporates "indirect" costs associated

---

[10] For a more detailed explanation, see Delucchi, 2000.

[11] Note that, due to the mass of carbon in a CO_2 molecule, a $1-per-ton tax on CO_2 is the same as a $3.67-per-ton tax on carbon.

[12] $58 = $44.85 (local environmental costs) + $0.15 (oil production costs) + $13 (climate change costs under proposed policies); $2.52 = $0.15 (oil production costs) + $2.37 (climate change costs based on damage estimates).

with oil consumption—for which other policy instruments are preferable and an oil tax would be second best. The low estimate excludes these costs.

Macroeconomic Disruptions and National Security. Consuming oil creates or exacerbates economic and political threats to U.S. national security. In addition, there are costs related to maintaining military forces to reduce these risks to U.S. security.[13]

Consumption of oil creates two major economic risks to the United States. One, an abrupt fall in the global supply of oil would result in a surge in the world market price. Because refined oil products are an important input to economic activity in the United States and a sharp price increase disrupts U.S. economic activity, several economists argue that past price surges precipitated economic recessions (Brown and Huntington, 2010). A surge in oil prices triggered by instability among oil exporters or an embargo would threaten U.S. security through the economic disruption it would entail.

Two, because the United States is a net importer of oil, large increases in U.S. consumers' oil payments associated with shifts in oil prices—or because of deliberate reductions in supply by major exporters—result in a shift in the terms of trade, reducing the value of U.S. income and assets. Although economic in nature, a large shift in payments reduces resources within the United States to pay for the Department of Defense, the Office of the Director of National Intelligence, and other efforts to make the United States secure.

Oil consumption, especially of imported oil, has been linked with multiple political threats to U.S. national security. These include the following:

- the potential of major oil exporters to manipulate exports to influence other countries in ways inimical to U.S. interests
- the potential for competition for oil supplies to exacerbate international tensions or disrupt international oil markets
- the effect of higher revenues from oil exports on the ability of "rogue" oil exporters, such as Venezuela and Iran, to thwart U.S. policy goals
- the potential role that oil export revenues can play in supporting terrorist groups.

Among these linkages, embargoes on exports of oil (and natural gas) have been unsuccessful in changing policies of nations that were targeted by an embargo (Crane et al., 2009). As long as oil is a globally traded commodity, oil-exporting nations cannot successfully target specific countries because importers can purchase alternative supplies on the global market.

Crane et al. found that higher oil export revenues have enhanced the ability of certain states, such as Iran and Venezuela, to pursue policies contrary to U.S. interests. However, the importance of donations from individuals and charities in oil-rich Middle Eastern states for financing al Qaeda and its affiliates has declined as terrorist groups have increasingly turned to crime to finance their attacks. Moreover, the costs of perpetrating a terrorist attack are so small ($15,000 to $500,000) that even a substantial fall in Middle Eastern oil revenues would not affect al Qaeda's ability to raise sufficient funds to finance its operations.

Some scholars have attempted to calculate these national security costs. Brown and Huntington (2010) estimate the additional costs associated with importing oil from unstable states at $2.35 per barrel on domestic oil and $4.60 per barrel on imported oil (both in 2009 dol-

---

[13] For a more detailed discussion of the relationships between U.S. oil consumption and U.S. national security, see Crane et al., 2009.

lars). If we assume that these estimates are accurate, then a $2.35 oil tax on all oil consumption combined with an additional tariff of $2.25 ($4.60 – $2.35) would internalize the external economic costs associated with oil consumption.

Costs of Defending Foreign Sources of Oil and Transit

Beginning with President Carter, ensuring the security of oil supplies and global transit of oil has been officially declared as a vital interest of the United States. It is a prominent element in U.S. force planning. If this mission were to disappear, the United States would almost certainly reduce some of its active-duty forces, although not all the forces engaged or earmarked for operations to protect oil supplies would be dropped from the force structure. Some of the forces included in planning for this mission are included in plans for defending U.S. interests through other missions.

Crane et al. (2009) estimate how much might be saved from the Department of Defense budget if the mission to protect the supply and transit of oil were to be eliminated. Crane et al. put together two estimates of these potential savings. The first analyzed savings from the post–Cold War drawdown, once the mission to defend Europe from the Soviet Union disappeared. Crane et al. used this analogy to estimate potential savings in forces that have been assigned to U.S. Central Command (CENTCOM), if the oil mission were to disappear. Using this approach, Crane et al. estimate total potential savings of $75.5 billion per year in 2009 dollars.

They also use a top-down approach to generate a second estimate of this cost. They estimate the share of effort in each combatant command dedicated to defending the supply and transit of oil. After dividing defense spending into core (fixed) and noncore expenditures, Crane et al. estimate potential savings in force structure and costs if this mission were to disappear. They find that $91 billion could be saved annually. The bottom-up and top-down estimates represent 12 percent and 15 percent of the 2009 U.S. defense budget, respectively.

These estimates are perforce approximations. Nevertheless, they serve to help bound these costs. They suggest that the cost of forces associated with protecting oil resources is neither $29 billion annually (a lower-bound estimate from Delucchi and Murphy, 2008) nor $143 billion per year (Copulos, 2007)—two numbers that have appeared in the debate.

Monopsony Premium

The United States is responsible for approximately 22 percent of total world oil consumption; consequently, if the United States were to reduce oil consumption, it could affect the world price for oil. *Monopsony premium* is the term used by economists to describe the potential effect on world market oil price—and hence the average cost per barrel U.S. consumers pay—that the United States might have by reducing its consumption of oil (Brown and Huntington, 2010; Parry and Darmstadter, 2003). Leiby et al. (1997) find that the optimal tariff associated with the monopsony premium is between $3.30 and $11 (in 2009 dollars) per barrel. Tariffs at this level improve aggregate U.S. welfare by pushing down world market prices through declines in U.S. demand. Although such a tariff could improve U.S. welfare, it is not optimal from a global perspective, and we do not consider it in our calculations.

A Potential Tax Rate for Oil

In the preceding discussion, we identified government expenditures linked to oil that might best be covered by a tax on oil. We also listed costs on society imposed by the production and consumption of oil. In Tables 3 and 4, we show the amounts of revenue and tax rates at various oil prices that would be needed to cover these costs. Table 3 shows tax rates and revenues

Table 3
Percentage Tax Rates Necessary to Cover Expenditures on Transportation

Expenditure Item	Expenditure (billions of dollars)	Rate Needed (%) at Each Oil Price Point ($ per barrel)					
		$50	$60	$70	$80	$90	$100
Surface transportation	75.00	21.9	18.2	15.6	13.7	12.1	10.9
High-speed rail	8.33	2.4	2.0	1.7	1.5	1.3	1.2
Air travel	10.82	3.2	2.6	2.3	2.0	1.8	1.6
Total	94.15	27.4	22.9	19.6	17.1	15.2	13.7
Charge per barrel[a]	13.72						

NOTE: All calculations are based on total 2009 U.S. consumption of 6,865,650,000 barrels of oil or oil equivalent. The numbers below each per-barrel oil price indicate the percentage of the price of a barrel of oil that each expenditure category would constitute.

[a] Indicates the total expenditures divided by total consumption in 2009.

Table 4
Percentage Tax Rates Necessary to Cover Externalities and Other Associated Costs

External/ Associated Cost	Cost (billions of $)	Rate Needed (%) at Each Oil Price Point ($ per barrel)					
		$50	$60	$70	$80	$90	$100
Production externalities	1.03	0.3	0.3	0.2	0.2	0.2	0.2
Climate change	16.27	4.7	4.0	3.4	3.0	2.6	2.4
National security[a]	23.85	7.0	5.8	5.0	4.3	3.9	3.5
Defense spending	83.25	24.4	20.3	17.4	15.3	13.6	12.2
Total	124.40	36.4	30.3	26.0	22.8	20.2	18.2
Charge per barrel[b]	18.12						

NOTE: All calculations are based on total U.S. 2009 consumption of 6,865,650,000 barrels of oil or oil equivalent. The numbers below each per-barrel oil price indicate the percentage of the price of a barrel of oil that each expenditure category would constitute.

[a] Calculated by multiplying 2009 oil consumption by the average internal and external costs of consuming oil given in Brown and Huntington, 2010.

[b] Indicates the total expenditures divided by total consumption in 2009.

needed to cover total federal transportation-related expenditures. We estimate the total transportation expenditures at $564.9 billion over six years or $94.15 billion per year.

Table 4 provides our low-end estimate of total external costs. We include climate change costs in Table 4 based on the marginal cost estimates of climate change outlined above. We do not include other consumption externalities, as we assume that those costs will be internalized through other, more direct policies. Finally, for national security costs, we assume an average of costs associated with domestic and imported oil. These costs are levied on all oil consumption, roughly equivalent to the current fraction of imported oil.

In general, these costs are not new. Either they are currently being incurred by society with no offsetting revenues from oil or they are being paid through other taxes. Thus, the illustrative tax rates in Table 4 would not impose additional costs on taxpayers, since society is bearing these costs, even if not explicitly. The tax on oil would substitute for existing taxes or reduce deficit financing used to pay for these expenditures.

In Table 4, defense spending associated with security and protecting oil resources constitutes $83 billion, or two-thirds of the total external and associated costs. Because this cost is not strictly an externality, the external costs associated with oil production and consumption total $41.15 billion. Recall that this is a lower bound on these costs.

Who Would Pay the Tax?

The most cost-effective place to collect a per-barrel tax on domestically refined oil would be at the refinery. For imports of refined oil products, the collection point would be at the port of entry. Both refiners and terminal operators would attempt to pass the cost of the tax along by raising prices for products produced from the oil, the most important of which are gasoline, diesel fuel, home heating oil, jet fuel, residual fuel oil (bunker fuel), and liquefied petroleum gases (see Figure 3). An oil tax would raise the price consumers pay for petroleum-based products. At the same time, some of the tax would be borne by producers, both domestic and foreign. In this section, we review the economic incidence of an oil tax and assess its distributional effects on consumers. We conclude the section by discussing how the oil tax could affect federal transportation appropriations and key implementation issues.

Distribution of the Tax Among Consumers, Refiners, and Domestic and Foreign Producers

We noted earlier that a tax of 17 percent on oil priced $72 per barrel, the price as of July 2010, would yield $11.52 per barrel in federal revenue and would be sufficient to cover the costs of proposed federal expenditures on ground transportation. Such a tax would replace current federal highway taxes on gasoline and diesel fuel. If a tax of this size were passed through to consumers—and if refiners passed the tax through uniformly across all refined oil products—the tax on oil would be equivalent to a tax of $0.261 per gallon of gasoline, $0.077 per gallon more than the current gasoline tax.

In the face of higher prices, consumers would reduce the quantity of these products they demand. How much they reduce demand depends on how badly consumers need these products or, in economic parlance, the elasticity of demand. In the short run, the demand for gasoline and diesel tends to be relatively inelastic; in other words, motorists and truckers have a hard time finding ways of reducing their consumption of these products. However, over time, demand is considerably more elastic, as motorists purchase more fuel-efficient vehicles or, in some instances, change commuting patterns or even move closer to their places of employment. In the short run (typically one year), estimates indicate that, if gasoline prices rise 10 percent, demand for gasoline falls only 1 percent or less (Goodwin, Dargay, and Hanly, 2004). However, in the longer run (typically five to ten years or more), a 10-percent increase in price could result in a 3-percent reduction in demand.

The demand for jet fuel and residual fuel oil (bunker fuel) is likely to be more elastic than demand for gasoline and diesel fuel (see, e.g., Dargay and Gately, 2010). A substantial amount

Figure 3
Composition of a Barrel of Oil in Terms of Refined Oil Products

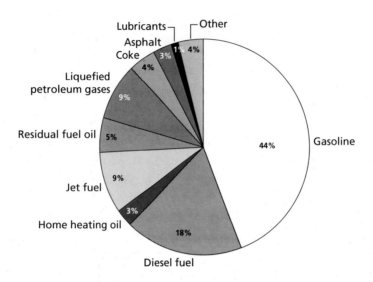

SOURCE: Energy Information Administration, 2010d.
NOTE: The numbers in the figure are the percentage of gallons in each barrel of oil that are turned into each product resulting from a typical refining process. "Other" products include kerosene and petrochemical feedstocks.
RAND OP320-3

of airline travel is discretionary, i.e., for pleasure. Increased costs of air travel stemming from increased prices for jet fuel is likely to result in a sharper decline in demand for jet fuel than for diesel fuel, which is used for commerce, or gasoline, since motorists find it necessary to make many trips. Residual fuel oil competes in some instances with coal or natural gas for industrial purposes. Its price is determined in great part by the prices of those substitutes because refiners have to price this residual product to sell. Refiners find it difficult to increase the price of this product.

Consequently, refiners do not mark up refined oil products uniformly: At any one time, margins on refined oil products are dictated in part by differences in the elasticity of demand (Considine, 2001). Because of these differences in demand, refiners might pass along more of the cost of a tax on oil on products for which demand is less elastic than on products for which demand is more elastic. Thus, gasoline and diesel fuel might bear most of the burden of an increase in the price of a barrel of oil because demand for these products is more inelastic. If refiners passed through a $12-per-barrel charge exclusively on gasoline, diesel fuel, and home heating fuel, the prices of these fuels might rise by $0.401 per gallon. As before, the net effect would be smaller if gasoline and diesel taxes were eliminated. However, passing costs through exclusively to a subset of fuels would be unlikely because jet fuel, lubricants, and other products would also bear some of the increased cost.

Higher prices would lead to a drop in the quantity of oil demanded. Although the short-term demand for oil is inelastic, so is the supply. Because most of the cost of extracting oil is incurred when drilling wells and building pipelines, once those investments are made, the variable cost of producing oil is modest. Consequently, producers do not cut back production when prices fall, as they continue to more than cover their extraction and refining costs. Because the supply of oil is inelastic, at least in the short run, small reductions in demand might result in larger falls in prices. This occurred in the first quarter of 2009. In the long run, however, oil supply is more elastic, and we would expect oil producers to respond to changes in the price of oil by adjusting production quantities.

The United States is a major consumer of oil, accounting for an estimated 22 percent of global consumption in 2009. The decline in U.S. consumption caused by an oil tax would lead to a fall in global demand, pushing down world market prices of oil. As noted earlier, imposing a 17-percent tax on oil priced at $72 per barrel is enough to cover projected federal ground-transportation expenditures. Such a tax would raise oil prices in the United States by $11.52 per barrel. However, if the tax replaces current taxes on gasoline and diesel, the net effect for consumers would be roughly equivalent to an increase in oil prices of $6.67 per barrel, a 9.3-percent increase in the price of oil because the increase in gasoline and diesel prices caused by the oil tax would be offset by the elimination of these taxes. Assuming a long-run price elasticity of demand of –0.3, over the long run, a sustained increase in oil prices of this magnitude might induce a decline in the amount of oil demanded in the United States by about 3 percent, or 535,000 barrels of oil per day. This decline in consumption would put some downward pressure on international oil prices. Using a model developed by Camm, Bartis, and Bushman (2008), we estimate that a decline in U.S. consumption of this size would push down world market oil prices by about 1.2 percent, or $0.83 when oil is priced at $72 per barrel. Under these assumptions, oil producers would pay 7.2 percent of the tax. The United States imported 54 percent of the oil and refined oil products it consumed in 2009. If that proportion were to continue, 4 percent of the tax would be paid by foreign producers of oil.

Refining and retail margins have been very tight in recent years because of excess capacity. Although margins widened in 2007 and 2008, the recent recession reduced margins again. Consequently, neither refiners nor retailers would be likely to pay a substantial share of the tax. Thus, according to the preceding analysis, U.S. consumers would pay about 93 percent of the tax.

Distributional Effects of an Oil Tax

The cost of an oil tax to consumers comes in two forms: direct and indirect. Direct costs include higher prices for gasoline or diesel paid for directly by purchasers. Indirect costs arise because of the increased cost of goods and services for which refined oil products are an input, such as plastics, or the increased costs of consumer goods sold in stores stemming from higher transportation costs.

Not all consumers will face the same burden from an oil tax. Households, whether categorized by income or geography, differ in terms of expenditures on oil-related products. For example, households that consume few oil-intensive goods, use public transit, and heat with electricity would see their energy costs rise less under an oil tax than households whose members drive to work and heat their homes with heating oil. Households in geographic regions where oil is used as a home heating fuel would face greater increases in energy costs than households whose energy comes from nonpetroleum sources.

The same holds true of businesses. Firms that use more refined oil products—such as shipping companies, for which petroleum-derived products constitute a larger share of costs—

would be disproportionately affected by an oil tax relative to businesses that consume fewer refined oil products.

Based on the data in Figure 3, if an oil tax were evenly spread across all refined oil products, most of the tax would fall on motorists (44.1 percent of the tax) and truckers (18.2 percent). People who heat their homes with fuel oil would pay 2.7 percent of the tax; airlines and the U.S. Air Force and Navy, 9.3 percent; and road-paving companies, 2.9 percent, although this would be passed on to government road-repair and construction budgets.

Energy costs are typically thought to be regressive, insofar as lower-income households spend a higher share of their income on energy products (Metcalf, 1999). Gasoline taxes have been shown to be at least weakly regressive based on gasoline expenditures as a share of total income (Poterba, 1991). Metcalf (1999) finds that energy taxes (e.g., carbon taxes or energy taxes, such as the British thermal unit (Btu) tax proposed by the Clinton administration) are regressive, though their indirect effects might be less regressive, especially on a lifetime income basis (Bull, Hassett, and Metcalf, 1994).[1] Households in different parts of the country are also affected differently by energy taxes. For example, in the case of a Btu tax, the burden of direct costs would be higher in the Northeast, but the indirect costs would be lower for households in the Northeast, with the combined effect being less total variation in incidence across regions (Bull, Hassett, and Metcalf, 1994).

An oil tax could be designed to reduce the burden on households by rebating tax revenue through reductions in other taxes that distort other markets. The potential benefits of this "revenue recycling" have been demonstrated in the context of energy or environmental taxes (Burtraw, Sweeney, and Walls, 2009). The regressive effects of an oil tax could be counterbalanced by reducing other taxes that are also considered regressive, such as payroll taxes. However, any revenue recycling would necessarily reduce the funding available for transportation and other uses because oil tax revenue would be offset by revenue losses from other taxes. Consequently, the total oil tax amount will need to take into account several competing uses.

Implications That the Proposed Tax Could Have for Transportation Appropriations

Assuming that the proposed tax per barrel on crude oil would be passed on to and indirectly paid by the consumers of the various refined oil final products, Congress would have to consider how the revenues might be apportioned across a variety of federal programs and geographic areas—and, implicitly, population groups. Although it is difficult to predict the outcome of a debate, it is possible to envision several alternative possibilities:

Link the Tax to the Highway Trust Fund
Even though some of the petroleum products that result from each barrel of oil are not ultimately used as transportation fuels or as asphalt, Congress might wish to eliminate the per-gallon motor fuel taxes and to direct the revenues from the proposed new tax entirely to the replenishment of the HTF. Conceptually, this might be the simplest approach. It also allows relatively straightforward calculation of an appropriate level for the new tax, since it would logically be set at a level that meets the estimated highway and transit programmatic needs or

---

[1]   A Btu tax is a per-unit tax on Btus, which are a measure of the heat content of energy.

negotiated levels of appropriations from the HTF. However, because other consumers of oil products would be paying part of the tax, the federal HTF could no longer be considered as being financed only by user fees.

Apportion the Revenue According to Its Use

Federal motor fuel taxes are currently considered to be "user fees." These taxes accrue exclusively to the HTF. Heavy truck registration fees and other charges levied against road users are also considered to be fees and flow into the HTF. In addition, a substantial proportion of the funds dispensed for transportation programs under current law must be spent in the state in which the revenue was collected. Today, each state is guaranteed it will receive from the HTF at least 92.5 percent of the funds it contributes. If the HTF were retained and existing user fees discontinued, it would seem appropriate that that proportion of the tax revenue that approximates the portion of petroleum consumption that eventually becomes gasoline and diesel fuel be designated for deposit into the HTF. Similarly, the proportion of each barrel of petroleum that becomes aviation fuel could be designated for use in the federal air-transportation program. The remainder of the revenue could then be contributed to the general fund. This approach would adhere to the concept of user fees but would be more complex to administer because it is difficult to precisely estimate the future proportions of the outcomes of the refining of petroleum, which, to some extent, can be fine-tuned to market conditions. It would also be more difficult to determine a geographic basis for apportionment of the funds than under the current program.

Abandon the Trust Fund in Favor of General-Fund Financing

During the past two years, Congress has used general funds several times to replenish the federal HTF; some have argued that the HTF and the concept of user-fee financing have outlived their usefulness. If Congress finds that the federal HTF has outlived its usefulness, the proceeds of the petroleum tax could flow into the general fund. Future highway and transit programs would be funded from general revenues. This would result in direct competition between transportation funding programs and all other general-funded programs of the national government.

Implementation

Setting the Tax

The key failure of current gasoline and diesel taxes is that revenues have not kept pace with the cost of building and maintaining federally funded highways, nor have they covered the external costs associated with oil. For an oil tax to be an effective means of raising needed revenues for transportation, it will have to be structured in such a way that revenues keep pace with costs. We also argue that such a tax could usefully tax producers and consumers of oil for external costs imposed on society by this product.

One way to rectify these problems is to set the percentage rate each year at a level that would cover appropriated expenditures and an estimate of external costs. Congress would appropriate funds for transportation; the percentage tax rate would be set so that the tax would be projected to generate sufficient funds to cover these expenditures and to cover external costs. For example, if the price of oil were $80 per barrel, a rate of approximately 40 percent would cover desired transportation expenditures (17 percent) and externalities (23 percent), under a hypothetical scenario in which these costs are additive.

Because oil prices fluctuate, the percentage rate would need to be adjusted so as to ensure that sufficient revenues are raised while cushioning taxpayers when prices spike. One way to achieve this goal would be to adjust the percentage rate quarterly, based on the average price of oil in the first two months of the previous quarter. For example, drawing on the example above, if the percentage rate had been fixed at 40 percent because oil prices had averaged $80 per barrel, and oil prices surged to $100 per barrel, the percentage rate would be cut to 32 percent in subsequent quarters because this rate would maintain revenues at the projected level.

Phasing In the Tax

In the previous section, we discussed potential shifts in prices on refined oil products and world market oil prices following the imposition of a tax. How these shifts will actually play out will depend on a wide range of market forces. Because of these uncertainties, Congress might choose to phase in an oil tax while reducing existing taxes on gasoline and diesel fuel. Such an approach would give policymakers time to determine how the tax affects refined oil product prices and therefore how the tax is being distributed across producers (domestic and foreign), refiners, and consumers. Using this analysis, Congress could make adjustments in terms of either expenditures or percentage rates.

Conclusion

There are compelling reasons to consider alternatives to existing motor fuel taxes in the United States. Current federal gasoline and diesel taxes—the largest contributors to U.S. federal transportation funding—are not indexed to inflation, have not been raised since 1993, and do not produce sufficient revenue to cover federal transportation infrastructure costs. An alternative, explored in this paper, is to replace existing fuel taxes with a single tax on oil and imported refined oil products. An oil tax would have appealing features: It is likely to be relatively easy to administer because it would be collected at the refinery or ports; it would spread the cost of transportation funding across a larger pool of users than current taxes do; it could account for the external costs associated with oil production and consumption; and it could be designed in ways to provide consistent funding for transportation infrastructure and other spending priorities. By tying tax rates to appropriated monies for transportation spending, and adjusting those rates to changes in world market oil prices, the tax would ensure that future revenues keep pace with transportation expenditures.

At the same time, imposing and implementing a percentage tax on crude oil would be challenging. Antitax sentiment is a major reason that existing federal fuel taxes have not been raised since 1994. Similar antitax political pressure could stall an oil tax proposal, although national security concerns might lend support to a tax on oil that other taxes lack. Phasing in might also help garner public acceptance for an oil tax. Ensuring that the transition away from motor fuel taxes toward a unified oil tax is gradual could make the tax more politically feasible. Setting the right amount for the tax is a key challenge, especially if one goal of the tax is to address the external costs of oil consumption. We have provided estimates of some of environmental, macroeconomic, and national security costs, but more detailed analysis would be needed to fully justify both a particular external cost estimate and the appropriate balance between revenue goals and reducing externalities.

Gasoline Prices and Federal Tax History, 1949–2008

Table A
Gasoline Prices and Federal Tax History (1949–2008)

Year	Unleaded Regular		Federal Gasoline Tax	
	Price (nominal) ($)	Price (real) (%)	Nominal	Tax/Price (%)
1949	0.27	1.64	0.01	4
1950	0.27	1.62	0.01	4
1951	0.27	1.54	0.02	7
1952	0.27	1.52	0.02	7
1953	0.29	1.57	0.02	7
1954	0.29	1.58	0.02	7
1955	0.29	1.55	0.02	7
1956	0.30	1.54	0.02	7
1957	0.31	1.55	0.03	10
1958	0.30	1.48	0.03	10
1959	0.31	1.47	0.03	10
1960	0.31	1.48	0.04	13
1961	0.31	1.45	0.04	13
1962	0.31	1.42	0.04	13
1963	0.30	1.40	0.04	13
1964	0.30	1.37	0.04	13
1965	0.31	1.39	0.04	13
1966	0.32	1.39	0.04	13
1967	0.33	1.39	0.04	12
1968	0.34	1.35	0.04	12
1969	0.35	1.33	0.04	11
1970	0.36	1.30	0.04	11
1971	0.36	1.26	0.04	11

Table A—Continued

Year	Unleaded Regular		Federal Gasoline Tax	
	Price (nominal) ($)	Price (real) (%)	Nominal	Tax/Price (%)
1972	0.36	1.20	0.04	11
1973	0.39	1.22	0.04	10
1974	0.53	1.53	0.04	8
1975	0.57	1.49	0.04	7
1976	0.61	1.53	0.04	7
1977	0.66	1.53	0.04	6
1978	0.67	1.46	0.04	6
1979	0.90	1.82	0.04	4
1980	1.25	2.30	0.04	3
1981	1.38	2.33	0.04	3
1982	1.30	2.07	0.04	3
1983	1.24	1.90	0.09	7
1984	1.21	1.79	0.09	7
1985	1.20	1.72	0.09	8
1986	0.93	1.30	0.09	10
1987	0.95	1.30	0.09	10
1988	0.95	1.25	0.09	10
1989	1.02	1.30	0.09	9
1990	1.16	1.43	0.09	8
1991	1.14	1.35	0.14	12
1992	1.13	1.31	0.14	12
1993	1.11	1.25	0.14	13
1994	1.11	1.23	0.18	17
1995	1.15	1.25	0.18	16
1996	1.23	1.31	0.18	15
1997	1.23	1.29	0.18	15
1998	1.06	1.10	0.18	17
1999	1.17	1.19	0.18	16
2000	1.51	1.51	0.18	12
2001	1.46	1.43	0.18	13
2002	1.36	1.30	0.18	14
2003	1.59	1.50	0.18	12

Table A—Continued

Year	Unleaded Regular		Federal Gasoline Tax	
	Price (nominal) ($)	Price (real) (%)	Nominal	Tax/Price (%)
2004	1.88	1.72	0.18	10
2005	2.30	2.03	0.18	8
2006	2.59	2.22	0.18	7
2007	2.80	2.34	0.18	7
2008	3.27	2.67	0.18	6

SOURCES: Gas tax information from "When Did the Federal Government Begin Collecting the Gas Tax?" 2005; price data from Energy Information Administration, 2010b.

Bibliography

Brown, Stephen P. A., and Hillard G. Huntington, *Reassessing the Oil Security Premium*, Washington, D.C.: Resources for the Future, RFF Discussion Paper 10-05, February 2010. As of January 21, 2011: http://www.rff.org/Publications/Pages/PublicationDetails.aspx?PublicationID=21018

Bull, Nicholas, Kevin A. Hassett, and Gilbert E. Metcalf, "Who Pays Broad-Based Energy Taxes? Computing Lifetime and Regional Incidence," *Energy Journal*, Vol. 15, No. 3, 1994, pp. 145–166.

Bureau of Transportation Statistics, "Table 1-32 U.S. Vehicle-Miles," undated (a). As of January 21, 2011: http://www.bts.gov/publications/national_transportation_statistics/html/table_01_32.html

———, "Table 4-23: Average Fuel Efficiency of U.S. Passenger Cars and Light Trucks," undated (b). As of January 21, 2011: http://www.bts.gov/publications/national_transportation_statistics/html/table_04_23.html

Burtraw, Dallas, Richard Sweeney, and Margaret Walls, "The Incidence of U.S. Climate Policy: Alternative Uses of Revenues from a Cap-and-Trade Auction," Resources for the Future, Discussion Paper 09-17-REV, 2009.

Camm, Frank, James T. Bartis, and Charles Bushman, *Federal Financial Incentives to Induce Early Experience Producing Unconventional Liquid Fuels*, Santa Monica, Calif.: RAND Corporation, TR-586-AF/NETL, 2008. As of February 1, 2011: http://www.rand.org/pubs/technical_reports/TR586.html

Considine, Timothy J., "Markup Pricing in Petroleum Refining: A Multiproduct Framework," *International Journal of Industrial Organization*, Vol. 19, No. 10, 2001, pp. 1499–1526.

Copulos, Milton R., *The Hidden Cost of Oil: An Update*, Washington, D.C.: National Defense Council Foundation, 2007.

Crane, Keith, Andreas Goldthau, Michael Toman, Thomas Light, Stuart E. Johnson, Alireza Nader, Angel Rabasa, and Harun Dogo, *Imported Oil and U.S. National Security*, Santa Monica, Calif.: RAND Corporation, MG-838-USCC, 2009. As of January 21, 2011: http://www.rand.org/pubs/monographs/MG838.html

Dargay, Joyce M., and Dermot Gately, "World Oil Demand's Shift Toward Faster Growing and Less Price-Responsive Products and Regions," *Energy Policy*, Vol. 38, No. 10, October 2010, pp. 6261–6277.

Delucchi, Mark A., *The Allocation of the Social Costs of Motor-Vehicle Use to Six Classes of Motor Vehicles*, Davis, Calif.: Institute of Transportation Studies, University of California, UCD-ITS-RR-96-3(10), December 1996.

———, "Environmental Externalities of Motor-Vehicle Use in the US," *Journal of Transport Economics and Policy*, Vol. 34, No. 2, May 2000, pp. 135–168.

———, *Summary of the Nonmonetary Externalities of Motor-Vehicle Use*, revised, Davis, Calif.: Institute of Transportation Studies, University of California, Davis, UCD-ITS-RR-96-03(09)_rev1, 2004. As of January 21, 2011: http://pubs.its.ucdavis.edu/publication_detail.php?id=156

Delucchi, Mark A., and James J. Murphy, "US Military Expenditures to Protect the Use of Persian Gulf Oil for Motor Vehicles," *Energy Policy*, Vol. 36, No. 6, June 2008, pp. 2253–2264.

Deutch, John M., James R. Schlesinger, and David G. Victor, *National Security Consequences of U.S. Oil Dependency: Report of an Independent Task Force*, New York: Council on Foreign Relations, 2006.

Energy Information Administration, selected crude prices, undated spreadsheet. As of January 21, 2011:
http://www.eia.doe.gov/emeu/international/crude1.html

———, Office of Oil and Gas, *Petroleum Marketing Monthly*, Washington, D.C., August 2, 2010a. As of January 21, 2011:
http://www.eia.gov/pub/oil_gas/petroleum/data_publications/petroleum_marketing_monthly/historical/2010/2010_08/pmm_2010_08.html

———, Office of Energy Markets and End Use, "Table 5.24 Retail Motor Gasoline and On-Highway Diesel Fuel Prices, 1949–2009 (Dollars per Gallon)," in *Annual Energy Review*, Washington, D.C., DOE/EIA-0384(2009), August 19, 2010b. As of January 21, 2011:
http://www.eia.gov/emeu/aer/txt/ptb0524.html

———, Office of Integrated Analysis and Forecasting, *Annual Energy Outlook 2011 with Projections to 2035: Early Release Overview*, Washington, D.C., DOE/EIA-0383(2011), December 16, 2010c. As of January 21, 2011:
http://www.eia.doe.gov/oiaf/aeo/overview.html

———, "Refinery Yield (Percent)," *Petroleum Navigator*, December 30, 2010d. As of January 21, 2011:
http://tonto.eia.doe.gov/dnav/pet/pet_pnp_pct_dc_nus_pct_m.htm

———, *Short Term Energy Outlook*, Washington, D.C., January 11, 2011. As of January 21, 2011:
http://www.eia.doe.gov/emeu/steo/pub/contents.html

Federal Highway Administration, U.S. Department of Transportation, "Annual Vehicle Distance Traveled in Miles, 1936–1995, by Vehicle Type and Highway Category," Table VM-201, April 1997. As of January 21, 2011:
http://www.fhwa.dot.gov/ohim/summary95/vm201.pdf

———, "Annual Vehicle-Miles of Travel, 1980–2008, by Functional System, National Summary," *Highway Statistics 2008*, Table VM-202, December 2009. As of February 2, 2011:
http://www.fhwa.dot.gov/policyinformation/statistics/2008/vm202.cfm

Goodwin, Phil, Joyce Dargay, and Mark Hanly, "Elasticities of Road Traffic and Fuel Consumption with Respect to Price and Income: A Review," *Transport Reviews*, Vol. 24, No. 3, May 2004, pp. 275–292.

Grogan, Tim, "Construction Cost Index," *Engineering News-Record*, Vol. 264, No. 11, 2010, p. 60.

Leiby, Paul N., Donald W. Jones, T. Randall Curlee, and Russell Lee, *Oil Imports: An Assessment of Benefits and Costs*, Oak Ridge, Tenn.: Oak Ridge National Laboratory, ORNL-6851, November 1, 1997. As of January 21, 2011:
http://www.esd.ornl.gov/eess/energy_analysis/files/ORNL6851.pdf

Metcalf, Gilbert, "A Distributional Analysis of Green Tax Reforms," *National Tax Journal*, Vol. 52, No. 4, 1999, pp. 655–682.

National Highway Traffic Safety Administration, "NHTSA and EPA Establish New National Program to Improve Fuel Economy and Reduce Greenhouse Gas Emissions for Passenger Cars and Light Trucks," undated fact sheet. As of January 21, 2011:
http://www.nhtsa.gov/staticfiles/rulemaking/pdf/cafe/CAFE-GHG_Fact_Sheet.pdf

Nordhaus, William D., "To Tax or Not to Tax: Alternative Approaches to Slowing Global Warming," *Review of Environmental Economics and Policy*, Vol. 1, No. 1, 2007, pp. 26–44.

Office of Management and Budget, "Table 2.4—Composition of Social Insurance and Retirement Receipts and of Excise Taxes: 1940–2015," Washington, D.C., 2011a. As of January 21, 2011:
http://www.whitehouse.gov/omb/budget/Historicals

———, "Table 8.7—Outlays for Discretionary Programs: 1962–2015," in *Historical Tables*, Washington, D.C., 2011b. As of January 21, 2011:
http://www.whitehouse.gov/omb/budget/Historicals

Parry, Ian W. H., and Joel Darmstadter, *The Costs of U.S. Oil Dependency*, Washington, D.C.: Resources for the Future, Discussion Paper 03-59, 2003.

Parry, Ian W. H., and Kenneth A. Small, "Does Britain or the United States Have the Right Gasoline Tax?" *American Economic Review*, Vol. 95, No. 4, September 2005, pp. 1276–1289.

Parry, Ian W. H., Margaret Walls, and Winston Harrington, "Automobile Externalities and Policies," *Journal of Economic Literature*, Vol. 45, No. 2, June 2007, pp. 373–399.

Poterba, James, *Is the Gasoline Tax Regressive?* Cambridge, Mass.: National Bureau of Economic Research, Working Paper 3578, January 1991.

Public Law 101-380, Oil Pollution Act of 1990, August 1990.

"When Did the Federal Government Begin Collecting the Gas Tax?" *Highway History*, Federal Highway Administration, U.S. Department of Transportation, June 2005. As of January 21, 2011:
http://www.fhwa.dot.gov/infrastructure/gastax.cfm